INTRODUCTION

Once upon a time there was ... a caveman. Every day after getting up the man had a clear choice: will I go hunting or will I be hungry? Since starvation is not pleasant, his wife would bitch if he did not, and his father had taught him to, he decided to go hunting. Day in, day out. Of course, in the course of the day he was confronted with more choices. Turn left or right? Rabbit or lion? Fight or escape? But then life was simple.

Later it became more complicated and complex. And where are we now? In one day we make not dozens nor hundreds, but thousands of decisions.

From very minor decisions (white socks or be embarrassed?) to very big ones (jumping for the train or divorce?). Life has thus become very, very busy and complicated. So many options. So little time (even though we live three times longer than did the caveman).

Since the second half of the last century there has been a lot of scientific research about how the brain works, and how we make decisions. Libraries have been filled with the results of those studies. The problem: they mainly explain how it works. Good to know. But what good does it do when you know exactly what happens in your brain when you have to make an important decision in your life? Much more useful is know how to make the right decision. And in as little time as possible. This is what "The Tosser's Method" will do for you.

"The Tosser's Method" described in this book is well known in the Netherlands as the "Dijkgraaf Methode". The method will not help you with the

The Tosser's Method

The easiest and most effective way
to make important decisions

JAN DIJKGRAAF

DEDICATION

For my dad,

who learned me

to keep it simple

CONTENTS

question whether you put horse or smoked beef on your biscuit in the morning. It will not decide for you whether you put a red or blue t-shirt on. And it will also not determine whether you want coffee or tea. Because these are things that are irrelevant in the context of real life. The method will help you with decisions that really matter and are important - where emotions are involved. Do I buy that house or not? Do I continue with the extramarital relationship or not? Do I tell my boss the truth, the whole truth, and nothing but the truth, or not?

This book will help you with decisions that really can be consequential for the rest of your life. When you finish reading it, you will think: is that all? Yes, that is all. You will also think: this method really works. Do you know why? Because it does! You too will make the right decisions in no time from now on. You will do that at home, in your private life, and at work. Or do you still think there is a difference between how we make decisions in our personal and professional lives? Do you think that we decide with our heart in our personal lives and with our brain in our professional lives? Forget it!

"The Tosser's Method" works everywhere. It saves you time and prevents worrying, headaches, sleepless nights, and feelings of despair. And that is... wonderful!

Eesterga, 2015

Jan Dijkgraaf

1 HOW PEOPLE DECIDE

We could get to "The Tosser's Method" right away, but it is a good idea to have a look at methods that have been around for a while and researched endlessly and are still being investigated (every month a new "brain book" appears). But we will only touch on these methods. Because in the end you will recognize them from your past, but you will not use them in the future. At least I hope so.

The first way of making a decision is: not to make one. Church going people know it as "Let God's water run on God's lands" meaning that you should not make a decision about anything. Quit your job? Well, you can do this any time later! Before you know it you'll receive a golden watch for your 25th anniversary or a kick in the butt and a one-way ticket to welfare because of redundancy upon reorganization.

In the eighteenth century the American politician Benjamin Franklin publicized the idea of using a list when confronted with a complex decision. He got a piece of paper, drew a line in the middle, and wrote the advantages of a decision on the left side and the disadvantages on the right. The idea was that if you have to make an important decision, you do not have all the advantages and disadvantages available at a glance, and therefore you cannot think in focus. (So if you thought you were original with your list, you're not, and by the way, the inventor of the mind map also was not.)

Listing the advantages and disadvantages at a glance was step one. Step two: reduce. Franklin deleted equivalent pros and cons. If two cons equaled three pros, he deleted all five. He would proceed in this way until in the end it became clearly visible which decisions would be most advantageous.

Sounds logical, right? Well, then here's the bad news already. Yes, this way of decision-making leads to a logical correct decision.

But what was the result of research in 2006 (a bit more our time than the eighteenth century) of Sheena Iyengar (known for the book *The Art of Choosing* among others)? That people who made decisions this way were less content with their decisions after half a year. We all strive more for being content than for 'scientific correctness'. At least I hope so.

There is also a theory stating that Benjamin Franklin and his followers had made hundred trillion lists with pluses and minuses, pros and cons, advantages and disadvantages, but these only serve as an alibi for decisions which the 'old' brain already made a long time ago (or eight thousandth of a second earlier).

Instinct, reflection, addiction, emotion, affection, and acting still win over reasoning and the intellect

Nobel prize winner Daniel Kahneman, who introduced psychology into economics, thinks that homo economicus does not exist. That is to say that the 'old' brain takes control in the background. The Dutch economist Paul Postma has added to that insight. His theory is that the hypothalamus (500 million years old) and the limbic system (200 million years old) always win over the cortex (hundred thousand years old). The first two control instinct, reflection, addiction, emotion, affection, and acting. The third controls reasoning and the intellect. Of course, over the last 200 million years a lot of knowledge has been added and we are not only acting on impulses (anymore), but pretending that our brain has completely been replaced by intellect is not wise, because it is not true.

Nevertheless, it is useful to know about how the brain works when you make a decision. There has been a lot of research about this since the second half of the last century, so we do not leave the work of the scientists untouched.

Geoffrey Leonardelli and Marilyn Brewer did a study with dots in 2001. The participants had to count dots and then were told that they belonged to the majority who estimated the amount too high or to the minority who estimated the dots too low. What happened? The participants of the study who belonged to the majority had more self-confidence than the participants who belonged to the minority. So: even though we think that we want to distinguish ourselves from the masses, the truth is that we want to belong to them. When we make a decision, we find what (we think) the masses will think to be important.

Walter Mischel did his famous marshmallow research in the sixties of the last century. Briefly: there is one marshmallow for a little boy. The scientist says that the boy has to walk a little and promises the boy two marshmallows when he returns, on the condition that the boy does not eat the marshmallow. But there is also a bell and when the boy rings the bell, the man will return immediately and the boy can eat the marshmallow, but will not get a second one. He only gets a second one if he waits patiently.

You already know it, right? Because you were once a child too. Even better, you still are. Only a few boys were patient enough to not ring the bell and wait. On average they rang the bell within three minutes. Conclusion: short-term gain always goes for gain in the long term. That applies to people of all ages. The modern brain understands that it is better to wait and waiting will not last an eternity, but the old brain acts impulsively and wants to eat the marshmallow as quickly as possible.

Another example that slams the idea that we are a kind of breathing computers? You ask - I deliver! The 'endowment effect'. First a short question. What do you have to pay for a coffee cup that is for sale for 19.95 dollar at Wallmart? Do you get it? I assume your answer is 19.95. (If not, you are weird). But that is not the value of the coffee cup as revealed the American economist Richard Thaler. His 'endowment effect' means that the coffee cup has a higher value

If we can choose between 300 dollar for sure and a 80% chance on 400, why do we choose the 300?

for someone who already owns it than for someone who does not yet own it. Translated to the context of private life, this also holds for your partner, so it is not necessary to be so jealous :-)

Ponder this: If you can choose between receiving 300 dollars for sure and 400 dollars at an 80% chance, what do you do? Indeed, the Israeli psychologists Daniel Kahneman and Amos Tversky discovered that we choose the sure 300 dollars. Even though that could also have been 33% more (with a big chance of 80%). But we do not like uncertainty. That has an impact on our decisions.

Another funny thing is that in 1955 the psychologist/sociologist Herbert Simon discovered that we do not strive for the maximum result when making decisions. What do we strive for then? Well, if somebody buys a new car, she or he will buy the car that fulfills his or her expectations in all areas (including the price). The car salesman can try to talk another 200cc into it, but he will not succeed (even though men lose their common sense in the car showroom). The other way around, the buyer will not negotiate another coco mat - good enough is good enough.

Simon noticed that making decisions happens according to rules of thumb. To give an example: it has to be a car of a well known brand and not the cheapest, but the second cheapest model. And yes, I work that way too. When I have done a lot of interviews, I always have my tapes transcribed. I put the job on a website for freelancers and choose the lady to whom I will give the job on the basis of a few rules of thumb. First rule: someone who has a vague application will not be selected. Second rule: from the rest I take the third cheapest. The third rule: I pay her a little more than she asks. Simple, effective, and of sound quality. (So if you are a parent, stop trying to stop the culture of getting grades that are just barely enough to pass...)

You might think that nobody has had the idea to

think of a mathematical formula for making decisions, because that is completely impossible. Wrong! There is a mathematical formula that can determine what you have to do: the EU model. EU does not refer to the European Union, but to Expected Utility.

The model has been developed by the Hungarian mathematician John von Neumann and the German economist Oskar Morgenstern. They stated that according to their mathematical model people choose the option that yields the highest expected return. The expected return is the sum of the values assigned to all options, weighed for the probability of each option to really occur. It sounds complicated, it is, and I will spare you the mathematical formula to prevent you from stopping reading too soon. According to Von Neumann and Morgenstern every choice different from the one that had to be made according to their model was irrational. But that is what we do: we make irrational choices, because we are people.

There is also a Dutchman who worked on this

In a combi-model there's also space for the heart and the gut – that's a lot more sympathetic already issue: social psychologist Ap Dijksterhuis. He presented a combi-model in 2007 that we should apply when we make complicated decisions. Dijksterhuis came up with a two-stage rocket. At first instance you have to carefully immerse yourself in the issue on which you have to make a decision. Sounds logical, right? And step two is even simpler: Dijksterhuis thinks you should get one night's sleep on it. Not necessarily literally, but what matters is that for a while you step away from step one and thinking about your 'problem'.

The method of Dijksterhuis is a lot more sympathetic than the methods of these economists and even mathematicians. Why? It also leaves space for two organs which cannot be taken into consideration in mathematical formulas and models: the heart and the gut. These organs - that make us different from computers - play an important role for people when making important decisions. And yes, business decisions too.

As for me, all that knowledge these gentlemen and lady have collected can be thrown out of the window from now on. Thanks for the effort, but we go to the next level of decision taking.

Are you ready?

3 THE TOSSER'S METHOD

Okay, enough waffle. Let's cut the crap. From now on you will (voluntarily) make every decision that is important to you on the basis of "The Tosser's Method". This method is so simple that you will not believe how come you have never used it before. You will even ask yourself whether I'm not nuts -or a conman.

Well, you never used the method because you did not know the art of KISS: Keep It Simple, Stupid! And no, I'm not nuts, nor a conman, I am just different from most people. Most people find it logical that with difficult decisions you also have to deal in

Logic says:

with 'difficult'

goes 'difficult',

otherwise it can

never be good

difficult considerations, have a hard time, have a feeling of difficulty in your head, heart, and stomach. With 'difficult' goes 'difficult', that is their logic, otherwise it cannot be good. It is my conviction, after half a century in this world, that it is exactly the other way around. If you are going to act difficult when confronted with decisions about matters that really affect you, you will not make progress. You have to make it as easy as possible. Well, that is exactly what "The Tosser's Method" does.

Firstly the short version. You ask yourself a question you can answer with 'yes' or 'no'. You take a coin. You call heads yes and tails no. You toss the coin. If the coin falls on heads, the answer to your question is yes. If the coin falls on tails, the answer is no. Now here is the crux: you are allowed to throw again. Do you want that or not?

The moment you have answered this question you know the real answer to the question you asked yourself. Because if you want to throw again, the other answer is the decision you will make. Because if you do not want to throw again, the current answer is the decision you will make. Do you get it?

Do you want the long version, to be sure? We will use an example for this. Suppose that your name is Jan and you become very unhappy with your job as a manager at a new TV station. Within four weeks of your first day at the job you want to hurt two very scary, sneaky, sly, psychopathic - and coincidently powerful - assholes (colleagues) even though you have never used violence in your entire life. There are not a whole lot of jobs up for grabs in your branch, so the question is: will you get yourself a heart attack to maintain your salary of 15 thousand dollars a month or do you have to take measures (with all possible risks for your mortgage of 600 thousand dollars)? Indeed an issue with a lot at stake. Money, house, health, ego, future… To name just five.

Normally an impossible decision to make. But not now. Jan asks himself the following question: do I quit tomorrow with all consequences or should I stay with all consequences? He gets a coin and decides: if it is heads I will quit and if it is tails I will stay. He tosses the coin and it is heads. That means: quit. Now Jan has one second chance. He is allowed to throw once again, but whatever the result will be, he has to do it. Does he want to do it or not? In short: if it becomes heads again, he will quit, and if it becomes tails, he will stay. The decision that Jan makes now is crucial.

Deep inside, in his head, heart, and gut Jan already knows which decision is the right one. "The Tosser's Method" only gives him the alibi to really make that decision. If deep inside Jan wants to quit with all consequences, he will see heads as a confirmation of being right. And rightly so! If Jan want to stay with all consequences, he will want to throw again.

But if he wants to stay, Jan won't throw a second time! Because what if it would be heads again? That

"The Tosser's Method" contradicts with your rational sense, feelings and everything else you can think of way "The Tosser's Method" would become an ordinary gambling game. It should never be that with issues of real importance. So if Jan is not satisfied with heads (quit), it automatically means that it will be tails (stay). (By the way, the Jan was me and I was very happy with the heads at one of the media I worked for...)

So the entire "Tosser's Method" consists of: one question (the issue), toss a coin (heads or tails?), one question of conscience (are you sure?), and one conclusion (that belongs to heads or tails).

I understand that everything in you rebels against this method. You have been taught to think well about the decisions you make, especially about important decisions. Then a smart ass comes along who says you should not think about these important decisions at all. It contradicts with your rational sense, past experiences, feelings, and what more you can think of. And you must be thinking: did I spend my well earned money on this? It cannot be that simple.

You think. But it is that simple!

Why? Well, I will explain it to you. You never make decisions about things that are really important

to you at the moment when the issue arises. There is always a process that takes place before the decision, and therefore there's time. Whether you consider a divorce, marriage, quitting your job, firing somebody, moving, stopping taking the pill, throwing your child with a drug addiction out of your house, starting an illicit affair, stopping your studies, or whatever, it will never be something that you will rush, because you are a sensible human being. If you are somebody who after seventeen years of happy marriage wakes up one day, opens the curtains, and says: "Well, let's divorce today", "The Tosser's Method" is useless for you. You will not take it (nor yourself) seriously.

With important issues it is always about decisions that have been around for a while in the back of your head. You already thought of the pros and cons a long time ago. You already felt what a yes and a no would mean for you. You might have discussed the issue with a good friend. You visualized it. You experienced the fears. For real, consciously. But mostly in your subconscious. The point is: you have to make a decision. And you give the power to a coin.

Of course I hear a "yes, but...". In the Netherlands I always hear a "yes, but…", why should that be different in any other country. The "yes, but...." concerns that with "The Tosser's Method" you disable your common sense. You throw a coin and subsequently decide on your gut feeling whether or not you like the result. If not, you take the other outcome.

Firstly, it is not true that you disable your common sense. I already said: with important decisions you never wake up to an issue that has to be resolved immediately. So your brain, your common sense have been involved for sure.

Secondly: your common sense cannot make decisions well. Take a divorce. You have three great

The only "yes, but…" concerns the quality of the question you ask yourself children, but you cannot stand your partner anymore. Not that you have to go to a Stay Away From Me institute (for men or women). But then suddenly you meet the (next) love of your life. Somebody with one great kid. What to do? With ration alone you will never get to a conclusion. Ration reminds: the house, the mortgage, the visitation rights, the new residence, etc. But there are also four great children who do not have any blame in this misery and who will be troubled by this. Your heart says: you only live once, so go with the new love. But we cannot do this to these children. It is an impossible dilemma. If you have dealt with that dilemma long enough and you jump from one choice to the other and you drive yourself crazy, there is only one option left in my opinion: "The Tosser's Method".

There is a very important "yes, but....". In my opinion it concerns the quality of the question. That is very important. Let us take a positive example: a marriage. There are many ways you can ask the question to use "The Tosser's Method".

"Do I continue with him/her?"

"Do I want to marry him/her?"

"Is this the man/woman of my dreams?"

"Will I marry him/her or live with him/her?"

"Is this for life?"

Five wrong questions. They are not closed enough. There are too many escapes. "Do I continue with him/her?" "Continue" with someone - that was not the question. You can do that without marriage. Or as good friends. Or as business partners. "Do I want to marry him/her?" Suppose the answer is heads (yes). Does that mean that it will happen as far as you are concerned?

The Dutch writer Willem Elsschot in 1910 (!) wrote: "Between dream and act there are laws in the way and practical objections, and also melancholy, which nobody can explain, and which arises at night, when man goes to bed". The same for: "Is this the man/woman of my dreams?" If yes, so what? If no, so what? "Will I marry him/her or live with him/her?" is already a bit better, because it assumes a love connection under one roof. But it is too vague. It is not specific enough, because one important answer is missing. If you have answered yes, when? Now? In 2025? In 2042? In your coffin? And "Is this for life?" (Based on Luka Bloom's fantastic song *This is for life*) is a ruthless question. Whose life? When does it start? How does it start? You wanted to know whether or not you wanted to marry this gentleman or lady, yes or no?

So you have to phrase the question very specifically and provide a determination of time and an active verb so that you can only explain the answer in one way. "Will I marry X in 2015?" (Name and address are known at the editorial office, JD.) Will I = your action, not somebody else's. In 2015 = in 2015, not in 2016, not once. X = X, not Y or Z.

Since the correct question is crucial, I will add some examples.

The answer to "Will
I leave my current
employer?" is
always yes –
because you will
retire or die

About quitting your job. "Will I look for another job?" "Will I leave my current employer?" "Should I wait for my employer's proposal for contract cancellation?" Three times wrong. "Do I look foranother job?" is an entirely different question than quitting your job. And when? Tomorrow? Next week? Next century? "Will I leave my current employer?" Haha, loser! The answer is always yes. Even if you never quit your job. You will be fired or retire. Or you die. "Should I wait for my employer's proposal for contract cancellation?" Eh... the question was supposed to handle quitting your job or not. Not whether you know how to come up with a nice excuse to not take action. So the correct question is: "Do I quit before the beginning of next month?" Do I quit = action. Before the beginning of next month = determination of time. If yes, you deliver your resignation letter on the 30th or 31st. No matter what. If no, you do not. And yes, I know you might not have a new job yet. If that is an absolute condition for you (and your gut!), you asked the wrong question.

Not my fault!

Are you beginning to get it?

Let's take buying a house or not (because as you know, people have a preference for positives). "Do I want to buy that new house deep inside or not?" "Do I get such a good feeling about that new house that I picture myself living there?" "Should I wait with buying the new house until my old house has been sold?" Oh well, there we go again. "Do I want to buy that new house deep inside or not?" Eh... yes? And then? Deep inside I want to be a multimillionaire tomorrow. Or have a divine body. Or whatever. But what I want deep inside does not lead to any action. So, wrong question. Just as is this one: "Do I get such a good feeling with that new house that I picture myself living there?" Way too noncommittal! And what a waffle! You with your good feelings ... To do or not to do, that is the question. And what about "Should I wait with buying the new house until my old house has been sold?" Perfect question. Your brain says, nowadays hopefully, 100 percent yes! You are nuts if you want to own two houses while you can hardly sell a house at all! But apart from that, if you ask the question, you are also prepared to accept the answer "no" and to buy the new house. Or you will throw the coin again if it is tails (and consequently the answer is yes). But again, perfect question. Should I = action, until my old house has been sold = determination of time. Also a good question is "Will I sign the purchasing agreement for that new house tomorrow?" A bit simpler, same result.

I still want to say something about heads or tails. On Saturday afternoons I play an honorary soccer referee and I always ask the captain of the visiting team: "Heads or tails?" Never: "Tails or heads?" And it is the same with "Yes or no?" We always say yes first and then no. This also means that heads much more often means yes than no. Since I have written it, you are aware of it, but it is more important to be more aware of it.

The bad news is:
you cannot start
with "The Tosser's
Method" right
away, you first need
an important issue

Because a question you ask is in principle also positive. "Do I quit tomorrow?" "Do I move to the apartment of the illicit woman (or man) next week?" "Do I make a little one tonight?" You do not ask: "Do I not quit tomorrow?", "Will I not move to the apartment of the illicit woman (or man)?" or "Do I not make a little one tonight?" Does this mean something? No. Because when you ask a 'positive' question ("Do I call a divorce lawyer tomorrow?") and the answer is heads, you can simply decide that you are not happy with the answer. And therefore your answer will be no.

Can you start with "The Tosser's Method" right away? Unfortunately not.

The chances that you have an issue that really matters to you now are slim. And with trivia it does not work. Can you practice already? For example by already asking some minor things for future? "Will I divorce my husband/wife within fifteen years?" "Do I take a white Opel when I buy a new car in four years?" "Will I ever get a shoe lacing diploma?" No.

No, you cannot practice with those kind of questions. Why not? Because the real emotional connection with the subject is absent. In fifteen years you could be in a wheelchair and happy that your current husband or wife wants to push you around. Within four years the white Opel might not be part of the collection anymore. Within ever shoes with shoelaces might not exist anymore. Now we also mentioned the last criterion which a good question has to fulfill: the action must not be too far in the future. That would make it too noncommittal.

Finally, is it necessary that the question can be answered with yes or no? Or can it also be an either/or question?

It is not necessary that the question be answered with yes or no. And yes, an either/or question is also allowed. Though I still say: better if it's not. "Do I buy house A this week or do I buy house B this week?" "Will I live with X this year or will I marry X this year?" "Will I quit at the end of this month or will I wait until I am offered redemption money?" You (hopefully) get the feel of why this is not an ideal option: there are too many or too few variables. The question "Do I buy house A this week or do I buy house B this week?" excludes the possibility that you do not buy a house this week or another house - and that is odd. So there're too few options in the question. "Will I live with X this year or will I marry X this year ?" ==> same problem. Too few options, because you can also stay alone or fall in love with someone else. And with "Will I quit at the end of this month or will I wait until I am offered redemption money?" there are other objections: there is no end date. Therefore because of the second option, which might never occur, the question is too noncommittal anyway.

In relation to the preference for yes/no questions and not for either/or questions I remind you of the beginning of this chapter. Why make it hard if it can be simple? Keep It Simple, Stupid!

Moving on, here's the summary of "The Tosser's Method":

1. Ask a concrete question about an issue that affects you with the following conditions:

   a) it has to be possible to answer it with yes or no

   b) it contains an active verb

   c) it contains determination of time in the near future.

2. Get a coin, determine whether heads is yes or no and toss the coin.

3. Decide whether you are satisfied with the outcome. If yes, that is your answer, if not, the other option is your answer.

4. Act according to the result.

We have not yet discussed whether you will act according to the result of "The Tosser's Method". If you see it as noncommittal advice or - even worse - as a joke, your feeling will remember that a little bit better every time you get the coin. In that case it all becomes bullshit. My question would be: why would you waste your time on it then? If you love to toss a coin, become a referee. In all sports there is a huge shortage of referees, and it is good against a potbelly too.

Conclusion: only use "The Tosser's Method" if you are serious. It does not matter for me, because I already got the money (thanks!), but do it for yourself. This way there is always one thing that will help you with the really difficult decisions in your life ... the coin.

EPILOG

I have tested "The Tosser's Method" hundreds of times. With business issues and very personal issues. Therefore I was able to develop something that started as "give me a question and the coin will give you the answer" further and further.

It became clear that the right phrasing of the question was much more important than I thought initially. And also that the method only works when the person who asks the question is emotionally involved with the issue. And finally I also discovered that it only works if the person who asks the question is prepared to act according to what the coin says. A noncommittal attitude is killing.

Someone recently asked me if I really applied the method in my life. The answer is heads :-) Or in other words: yes. When I, the Jan who you met earlier when quitting that job at a TV station after four weeks, really had long lists of pros and cons for leaving and staying, was mindfucking all night long, and discussing the issue with my loved ones, I really threw heads on the question whether or not I should quit. I have never been as happy as back then (Monday 20 September 2010) seeing the face of our queen Beatrix on that coin.

One of the people who helped me to develop "The Tosser's Method" is the "coin girl" (hi Nicky!). She is from the younger generation and female and she also did the necessary fieldwork with her friends. If she had explained the method and formulated the question with her friend, it happened regularly that her friend said: "Oh, so I have to simply follow my gut feeling, because in my gut I already know for a long time which decision I have to make." Smart ass! If it were so easy, the coin girl would not have to talk about it with her friends, because they would have made the decision a long time ago. So "The Tosser's Method" is also useful for them, because it works as a much-needed kick in the ass.

Lots of luck with it! And most of all, with the rest of your life!

Jan Dijkgraaf

jan.dijkgraaf@gmail.com

ABOUT THE AUTHOR

Jan Dijkgraaf (1962, Rotterdam, the Netherlands) is a former editor in chief of several Dutch magazines and the free daily Metro. He now is a successful writer, columnist and business coach. His own company is called Buttkicken.nl.

Printed in Great Britain
by Amazon